The Divine Butterfly

Inspiration For The Journey To Your Purpose

The Divine Butterfly

Inspiration For The Journey To Your Purpose

Karen H. St. Hilaire

TABLE OF CONTENTS

TABLE OF CONTENTS vii

ACKNOWLEDGMENTS ix

INTRODUCTION 1

GREATER WHY 3

CLARITY 9

LIFE GOALS 17

ECIPROCITY 25

ESILIENCE 31

PATIENCE 37

CHOICES 44

DISAPPOINTMENTS...52

I AM… 58

ATTITUDE 65

O ORDINARY-NESS 73

MING...79

CRIFICES...85

BOUT AUTHOR..93

ACKNOWLEDGMENTS

A big thank you to my mom; my everything, Pauli. You have your way of pushing me through the good and bad times. You have walked with me throughout this journey with faith and a good side eye, and for that, I am eternally gracious.

Thanks to my butterflies: Tinayah, Jenee, and Kaleigh—the three young ladies that allow me to play mom when they are with me. They truly keep me grounded and happy.

Also to my cousin, Tricia, thank you for being a constant: whether we are climbing uphill or skipping downhill, I know I always have your back.

Thank you to all those who took out time to provide invaluable feedback as I embarked on this journey: Tomasina, you have been pushing me since high school, and I am eternally grateful for your (and Eric's) love and support. Fatima and Laura, you saw the light in me since graduate school, thank you for helping my flame grow and glow. My 'Special,' Jasmine, you gave this book life and poured prayer and encouragement into me throughout this journey, thank you, and I love you (you got next). Jocelynne (my ride or die), I appreciate you and our friendship. To Victoria, you are the best attorney and friend that I could ever ask for; I love you. To "The Squad," you know who you are, and you girls/guys rock. Thank you to my siblings and their families for being great. To Angela & Anthony at Therapy Wine Bar, thank you for allowing me to use your space as my sanctuary. TSquared Consulting; Tracy, your work on my brand has been inspirational, I am so grateful. Felicia Kinscy, you are my angel, you gave me access and I have never turned back. I am eternally indebted to you! A hearty skeewee to my beautiful sorority sisters.

Lastly, to the monarch butterfly that continues to push me to my personal greatness with silver spoons, I love and appreciate you.

INTRODUCTION

I remember the day I decided to host a tea party at my house for some of my girlfriends and classmates from grad school. The spread was small but tasty, and I served gourmet tea from Mighty Leaf and Pepperidge Farms Butter Cookies for them to gnash on. As we conversed about life and our plans for the future, the conversation turned into an inspiration session. Some of the ladies really needed a pep talk that would provide energy for the journey they were about to embark upon. New jobs, motherhood, quitting a job and going on a mission to find self. Some of the ladies not only found themselves in the conversation, but one, in particular, heard her inner voice for the very first time. The inner voice that comments on every aspect of our lives, she heard it, and it was a negative dialogue. I realized that some people just need some good support and a nudge—they need someone to be the wind behind their backs as they travel on the journey to personal fulfillment.

A few weeks later, one of the ladies that attended the tea party sent me a private message. In the message, she asked that I send some inspiration out into the universe on her behalf as she was ready to take a leap of faith, she was getting ready embark on what she believed to her life's work or her "purpose journey." I immediately understood what she meant without asking and was able to not only share an encouraging word about her being ready, but I also helped her create a meditative regiment with the mantra "I am enough."

As time passed, I realized that motivating and counseling others concerning their purpose journey is my life's mission—my purpose journey, hence this book.

1

One's purpose journey is the journey embarked on with the aim of achieving their predestined purpose in life.

Most people love butterflies because it signifies divine inspiration, confirmation, and validation of the choices that we are making with regard to our mission work. That is your journey's purpose—your personal mission work. You are destined to fulfill this task for balance to be achieved in the universe. This book is your Divine Butterfly.

The Divine Butterfly was written for everyone who is thinking about his or her life's purpose. It is also a guide for those who are in the process of doing their life's work. The objective of this book is to encourage the ones who are doing the work but are experiencing bumps on the road to fulfilling their purpose. These bumps can come in any form, and not exclusive to strained relationships, self-doubt, and even fatigue. The journey is never an easy one, to begin with, but it will be rewarding in the end. You get to experience the fact that you were created to be a blessing to people around you and the world beyond.

Within the pages of this book are life tools that will equip you with tactics, and ease you through stumbling blocks that will come your way on your journey to fulfillment in life.

You are never too young or old to start your life's work. It is indeed God's will at all times.

My prayer is that this book, *The Divine Butterfly:* Inspiration For The Journey To Your Purpose blesses everyone who reads it.

I look forward to reading your feedback about this reading experience. Please share your comments using the hashtag: *#thedivinebutterfly* on your social media platforms.

GREATER WHY

This book requires you to set aside time to focus on your goals and countenance. When doing your life's work, the act takes a toll on your physical, mental and spiritual well-being, so, we must develop our mental muscle in order to stay the course. You will be required to do some personal autopsies, as well as meditations. However, first, I want you to understand why you are doing these exercises and how rewarding it will be.

WHAT IS MEDITATION?

Meditation is the practice of concentrated focus on a sound, object, visualization, breath, movement, or attention itself to raise the awareness level of the present moment; reduce stress; promote relaxation, and enhance personal and spiritual growth. Meditation benefits people with or without acute medical illness or stress.

Studies have shown that individuals who meditate regularly experience lesser anxiety and depression levels. Other reported benefits of meditation include more enjoyment and appreciation of life, and improved relationships with others—meditation produces a state of deep relaxation and a sense of balance or equanimity.

Various techniques of meditation have been practiced for over a millennium. Originally, meditation was intended to develop spiritual understanding, awareness, and direct experience of ultimate reality. The many different religious traditions in the world have given rise to a rich variety of meditative practices.

These include the contemplative practices of the Christian religious orders, the Buddhist practice of sitting meditation, and the whirling movements of the Sufi dervishes. Although meditation is an important spiritual practice in many religious organizations and spiritual traditions, it can as well be practiced by anyone regardless of their religious inclination or cultural background to relieve stress and pain.

I remember the first time I meditated, it was a happenstance: I thought I was just sitting there, listening to the wind; the chirping birds, and letting my mind wander. Quite on the contrary, I was immersed in a moment of surrender—I was in a zone, and I was meditating. The last time I visited Martha's Vineyard, I was able to meditate with nature, and that was mind blowing. The wind, birds, rustling of leaves makes it an awesome sitting experience. I was able to visit Menemsha and meditated as the sun was setting into the horizon. I stood on the cliffs and listened as the waves hit the shore and actually set my breathing the match the sound. I was able to create the "Vision Alchemy" cards during my meditative sessions on Martha's Vineyard.

I have a one-hour commute every day from my home to the office, and I take the train—public transport being the easiest means of transportation for me. I am claustrophobic, and getting on the train every morning during rush hour means that I will experience congestion in the tunnels. I especially suffer from anxiety attacks each time the train stops in the tunnels. I also have a phobia for being crushed and having bodies pressed upon me first thing in the morning, but I live in New York, and that is part and parcel of our daily rush-hour commute.

After years of anxiety attacks, frustration and discomfort, I learned to be still at the moment—I created a go-to playlist, I have e-books audio books and sometimes a hard copy of a novel in my tote bag. I also have two puzzle games on my phone that I play during my commute. So, whenever faced with this routine, I will get lost in the music and concentrate on the game. As time went on, I began to look forward to my commute.

WHY BUTTERFLIES

Butterflies are known to bring good omens: around the world, people view the butterfly as a representation of grace, endurance, change, hope, and life.

In the Native American culture, the butterfly is a symbol of change and joy—the butterfly was considered a miracle of transformation and resurrection. They are a deep and powerful representation of life. Many cultures associate the butterfly with our souls: Christians believe that butterflies are a symbol of resurrection. Some cultures believe that the butterfly is here to guide us on the journey to freedom and ascension.

Anytime a butterfly comes into my personal space, my hearts skips a bit, and I smile because I believe that I am being blessed. I sense a type of synchronicity with the butterfly and understand the message. I have curated my meditative space with butterflies because their nature is reflective of how I want my life's journey to be—peaceful, rewarding and a heck of a learning experience.

At the end of every chapter of this book, I suggest you do a "Butterfly Meditation." This activity will allow you to focus on your personal growth. Also, each time you are on a page with the mention of the butterfly meditation, I want you to take some time and meditate anytime, from maybe five minutes to an hour. When you do, I need you to reflect each statement. After each meditative session, I have provided you with some blank pages where you can jot down your thoughts. If you are reading the eBook version, you can make use of your eBook reader's notepad to type in your thoughts.

It is important that you document your growth; it is important that you chronicle the journey because it will be rewarding to look back and understand every step you took that got you to a place of greatness. You will be able to assess your growth, weak moments and relive some successes that allowed you to re-charge and push forward. Meditating will be one of the ways that you will get around many hurdles.

SETTING THE ATMOSPHERE

A private spot where a peaceful atmosphere vis-a-vis tranquility is domineering is an important space you can have in your home for relaxation, meditation, and prayers. Identify a space in your home that can serve as your "calming corner." This is a space away from all the fuss; space where you can get to the core of your creativity. You can sit in that space to download thoughts, create new programs/processes for executing your work.

My sacred space is in my bedroom: in one corner where I have arranged a small table. On this table, I have my Vision Alchemy cards that I pull for focused meditation. I also have a candle, incense, prayer beads and a pink Buddha statue. I take pride in the time that I spend with myself and with God. My meditative moments are vulnerable conversations with God.

With candles lit, a soothing playlist playing in the background and my mala in hand, I begin to pray—I ask a question or make a statement that requires a response. Getting an immediate answer or sign as a result of prayer is not always immediate. But don't lose focus of what you are trying to accomplish. In time, you will get some insight that will serve as an answer to your prayer.

You should do what works for you. Just do something that works for you if setting up a space isn't conducive to your living arrangements.

List of things that can enable a meditative moment:

- Yoga

- A dancing session

- You can play an instrument

- Listen to meditative music

- Take a walk

- A morning jog

All of these things and more can be used to ease into your meditative moment, what you choose is entirely up to you and what makes you best comfortable. Just be intentional.

BUTTERFLIES RESPONSE

Using your trusty journal or the notes function in your eBook, note down the responses you receive during your meditative exercise in the following blank pages.

Divine Butterfly Expectation

What do you expect to get from this book?

*Embark on this reading journey with expectation.

Chapter 1

CLARITY

Sometimes, narrating a divine revelation can be a tad confusing. A divine revelation is a message that is received from the Divine or God. Sometimes it comes in the form of a dream or even a random conversation with a stranger. You will always know what it is because of the feeling that comes with it. You will experience a stirring in your Spirit. As you work on your purpose journey (could be building a school for underprivileged kids in rural areas), you will gain some more clarity which will provide you with insights on how to better communicate your purpose journey with interested parties or partners. The words used to define your life's work and journey are important, and you have to speak with much clarity because you want people to get it. Expressing yourself clearly helps others to understand you, which in turn prevents misinterpretations. Through being articulate about your purpose journey, people will not misinterpret your words, works, or actions other than the way that you intended. You must keep in mind that the divine revelation was given to you and the vision must be narrated by you and no one else.

Of course, you will meet people who can offer guidance or assistance as you build the narrative for your business, but do not lose sight of the fact that the baby is yours to nurture. You want all translations or transmissions about you and your work to be dictated by you. All talking points should be as you shared it in with your vocabulary.

If you are sharing your vision with your life-long friends and family who know you well, much explanation may not be required. But, that does not mean that you need not be elaborate when giving account. They may be able to read between the lines and call you to the carpet on fluff or nothing of substance, but bear in mind that there is a percent chance they might misapprehend your narrative.

Your purpose journey is not just some bright idea: this is your life's work you are talking about, and there is no o;ther route except one of clarity and transparency. Another substantial reason to discuss this vision with family and close friends is that it allows you to rehearse for the big stage. Feedback from the public may come with varying degree of character assessments and misguided opinions. People believe what they see and hear at first impact without waiting for explanations. Discussing with your friends and family about your work will help you build your narrative to near perfection. The productive conversations you have with your close circle about your existing business or brand (reputation) should be detailed as well.

I have met with individuals who take their life's purpose as just another hobby: "I love teaching children" or "I love cooking for seniors, it makes me feel great." These examples as mentioned earlier are not just hobbies and should be taken seriously because they are indeed a life's purpose. A fulfilled work life and million-dollar brands have been conceived from these so-called "hobbies." If this is same with you, then you already have the narrative mastered, and your next goal should be centered on a building a consistent brand and business.

Your thoughts and interactions must be consistent—you should do a self-assessment.

You may be thinking: "What does that look like?" or "How does one assess their inconsistencies?"

Here are some examples:

- "What do I know?"

- "What don't I know?"

- "How can I learn the things I need to know?"

- "Who can I contact to point me in the right direction?"

Eventually, you will realize that being transparent and upfront about your shortcomings puts you in the winning circle.

I remember when I was working hard to create a platform for my business. I had to ask myself (and respond to) some tough questions. "Who am I to do this work? Will people take me seriously? How am I going to work and walk in a syncopated cadence?" All of these things were extremely difficult to deal with. The reality became that I had to curb my expectations for many things and people. I had to focus on the walk and the talk. I had to endure the bumpy terrains while reflecting on the divine deposit. In short, I had to stay the course in a way that was mindful of all that was happening around me.

I conducted some research, stepped into unfamiliar territory by assimilating with those who may not look like me, but did something somewhat similar to what I was doing. My circle got smaller and more defined. It included trusted friends and truth talkers; I call them my 'holy of holies' or the HOH. These individuals have helped me to refine my talking points, speak in my truth and own my craziness. They afforded me the opportunity to be more clear and concise when talking about this work of purpose that I do daily.

If you are the type of individual who tends to speak in allegories, then you will most likely get misinterpreted more often than you would like. Speaking in figuration is synonymous to "you try and figure out what I am saying." This gives someone the opportunity to add his or her thoughts to your narrative, and that can give everything a whole new meaning. Communicating using metaphors leaves your message "subject to interpretation" by the reader or listener. The public should not be subjected to having to interpret what you mean unless that is your intention. If that is the case, you should have an ulterior motive or plan of action. Always think about how your words fall on the ears of others. How your words are construed is something you should reflect on before you speak to certain individuals. Let's take a child, for example, your words are literal in their world—if it does not make sense to them and they think that you are twisting words or being duplicitous, they will call you out, and you will be forever labeled a falsifier.

Be consistent in words and action.

Perception is their hard reality. Children do not fact-check; they read your disposition. Be clear about what you are saying.

Divine Butterfly Meditation

What Do You Know?

What Don't You Know?

Divine Butterfly Meditation

Chapter 2

LIFE GOALS

Life Goals are the projects that are personal to you and by extension, your legacy in the world. Your life goals can be as simple and short-term as waking up early or eating healthy, or as large and long-term as building schools in low-income areas. Life goals allow you to leave an imprint in the universe. If you stop to look at your track record of projects that only you know exists, and the steps are incomplete, then you are not working on your goals. It is at this time you should take a loving minute to have that little self-talk.

The self-talk should go like this:

- Is that a realistic goal?

- What's the ultimate plan?

- Who do I aspire to be like or compete with?

For some people, the life goals are as simple as being able to declutter their personal space. There are steps that you can put in place to help you achieve this goal. It could be as simple as placing bins in certain areas to store clothing or books or anything that could potentially become a dump item and cause clutter.

In life work, your goals may be to accomplish a few things one step at a time. Let's use the idea of starting and growing a business that will allow you to do the work that you have been purposed to do. It would be a great idea to list the things that you would need to do in order to get your business off the ground or to grow into a bigger entity. Here are a few examples.

- Register your business with the State

- Get training on how to do accounting or PowerPoint

presentations to move your business along.

- Survey social media trends that will work for your business and pull the clientele that you need in order to be successful.

It may also mean that you need to engage in paid media and or hiring an intern or part time help to get to the level of success that is on your goal list. One of the big hurdles that you will face is trying your end goals with strangers. They will have a hand in curating the process, and that may not end the way that you envisioned.

~

Steve Jobs, the founder of Apple and creator of all things iTech, was a habitual goal setter. He always had short-term and long-term goals. These goals were said to give him direction and serve as milestone checkpoints on his rise to industry domination. Even when the CEO that he hired ousted him from Apple, he set a goal to return to the top and remain there until his demise. He created a company NEXT that was subsequently acquired by Apple and ushered back his return to his beloved company.
He had goals.

Do you remember the day you heard about or purchased your first Apple product?

Let's use an iPhone for purposes of this chapter.

When Steve Jobs created the iPhone he wanted individuals to have the ability to make and receive phone calls; listen to music; browse the Internet, and access their email.

He also wanted to provide an office in your pocket so-to-speak. The journey to creating the company and these products was far from easy. However, life allowed him to grow this small business from a garage entity to one of the top technology conglomerates in the world.

Setting goals in your life allow you to see your missteps and these goals can be the ultimate lesson of failure and success on your journey.

Nothing will ever be easy, but avoiding costly and timely pitfalls can be a lifesaver.

Harvesting is an exciting time for anyone who has put in hard work and had to wait for the rewards. Reaping the benefits of your labor gives you unspeakable joy. The joy is ticking off the boxes next to the bucket list that is a part of your life goals. Think about it. Your bucket list consists of things that you want to accomplish within the space of your time on earth. For example, I am afraid of heights; water over my head, and I cannot swim. I decided that a major life goal to add to my bucket list was to do a zip lining. Why? Simply because it would help me concur my fear of heights, water and not being in control. I knew that I would never go through with it because I can be a coward when it comes to my phobias. Fortunately, last summer, a friend called and asked that we go on a "girl's day trip." I met up with her, and we went zip lining. I had to ride up a gondola—dangling in the air. I had two panic attacks. Then I zipped on three different courses: more panic attacks. But at the last course, I allowed my mind to wander off to picture huge lakes, trees changing colors, and my feet dangling over that water. This goes without saying I will never do this again, but the silver lining was that I was able to check something off my bucket list.

Simple should be harder than complex.
Steve Jobs

Some people tend to pass the buck and have someone else do the work while they sit back and WAIT for the benefits to pour in.

But, that is not and will not be you because you are FOCUSED and ready to work. Stay the course.

Tick the goals of the list one by one and celebrate in your own way.

Divine Butterfly Meditation

What are your "Life Goals"?

*How are you working
on these goals?*

Butterfly Response

Chapter 3

RECIPROCITY

In social psychology, reciprocity is a social rule that says people should repay, in kind, what another person has provided for them: that is, people give back (reciprocate) the kind of treatment they have received from another. By virtue of the rule of reciprocity, people are obligated to repay favors, gifts, invitations, et cetera. In the future—if person A receives a gift on their birthday from person B, a reciprocal expectation may sway person B to do the same on the person A's birthday. This sense of future obligation associated with reciprocity makes it possible to build continuing relationships and connections. Reciprocal actions of this nature are relevant to social psychology as they explain our everyday actions.

Reciprocity is not only a strong determining factor of human behavior, but it is also a powerful method for getting someone to help you when you need help.

Through capitalizing on reciprocity, I do not want to believe that we take advantage of people: I am a big believer of depositing into folks and their endeavors. This means that when I am ready to withdraw, it would not be a loan. Withdrawing means that I'm in need of a favor, service or connection from a person, I have sowed into them at some point in time, and they won't hesitate to assist me as I work in accomplishing my goals. There are times when I am prepared to ask for a favor and folks come up dry, and it bothers me. I take those times as lessons learned. My mom likes to say, "Just because they did it to you does not mean you have to do it to them." OK!

There will be occasions that you may have to share your gifts and talents as payment for access to a room of possibilities or to certain people. It can also be access to a possible opportunity in the future. It does not mean that you continually give away your services just because you feel it is the right thing to do. You don't want to be used by anyone or stifle your possible income by granting favors to everyone. I created my own formula for self-preservation, I started keeping a record of my favors. The terrible part is that I became ruthless when I realized that I am being taken advantage of with a smile. People ask for favors in a way that pulls at your heartstrings, and you feel guilty saying no to them. It may take you a while to see people for who they really are, but the lesson is to acknowledge it and then make the right decisions for yourself. Yes, you may get caught in a few quagmires, but such is the game of "give and take." Put on your full armor and put in the work.

One weekend I had the pleasure of walking down the street with my colleague, Sir, who felt the need to greet everyone who walked past him. Since this is Sir's nature, there was nothing wrong with this action. I, on the other hand, being the consummate assessor noticed that less than half of the people greeted, actually responded. My next comment was to simply say, "you might want to stop greeting strangers." My reaction to the lack of reciprocity was defensive since I noticed that more than half kept quiet.

We then had a great conversation about reciprocity, and Sir mentioned that some people "just don't care about it. It is no biggie for them to accept an act of kindness and keep it moving. We can label it 'entitlement' or we can call it 'rudeness'—no matter what we call it, folks just don't care." *On the way back to home, I was able to reflect on the entire situation. Some people did not respond verbally, but they did seem to be at ease for at least five seconds. Others looked in our direction and some just plain ignored us.*

Make it your business to be cognizant of your gratitude scale. It will work wonders for you in the future. If you are often showered with gifts, reciprocate one day (it does not have to be an exorbitant amount), it can be a "just because" gift, but watch the smile and the glow that will follow. I could go on, but you get it. Being a gracious and reciprocating is the cheapest and most memorable quality that you can afford a person.

While on this purpose journey, you will have to ask for some favors, and you are going to want folks to come through for you. Don't be alarmed by the amount of no's that you will encounter. Especially from those you have helped in the past. That all comes with the territory. Just practice equanimity, and you will be successful. Reciprocity can serve as your credit on file that can dictate how much help you stand to receive.

Divine Butterfly Meditation

How do you measure humility?

Butterfly Response

Chapter 4

RESILIENCE

Everyone has an opinion, it's part of our culture and people. Folks love to express their thoughts freely even when it is not wanted. Don't own it.

There will be diverse opinions from people on every aspect of your life regarding your decision to focus on your purpose journey. Folks will have advice, suggestions, and connections, and even offer to work for you; decide for yourself if you need it. Ask yourself some questions: 'does this advice help my business or does it even fall in line with what I am doing? Does this person project the energy that I require of myself and others when doing this life work?" You have to be resilient because doubt will always attempt to whip its way into the forefront of your mind.

Outside opinions can cause you to second-guess yourself. Sometimes, the takeover does not always have to be hostile. Just a nugget of doubt is potent enough to kill your dream. Opinions are similar to weapons of mass destruction.

Assassins are usually on a covert mission—they will blend into the group as a mole in order to make a successful hit. If the assassin has to infiltrate a group, they work tooth and nail to gain the trust of everyone in the group, including their target. This means they get really close to the person. The hit is always a surprise to the victim because the victim would invariably let their guard down. The assassin was patient enough and worked so diligently to get close. It will be the same for you. An assassin will not come for your life, but that person who is close to you may kill your spirit and drive to achieve your purpose in life. Their words will pierce the armor of your dreams because they know exactly where your soft spots reside. I am using the term assassin loosely, but you have an idea of where I am going with this. Sometimes our parents, spouses, and friends doubt some moves that we make because it is not in line with their expectations of us. It may not be in line with a plan that they had or with the societal norms as they know it. The negative response or push back can do a number on you as a person, and on the way, you move forward.

I remember the day I shared my future goals with someone that I was dating, and they laughed in my face. I stood there dazed because the person deposited a hefty dose of doubt into my spirit. After the laugh, the first comment made was "you are not going to make any money from that because folks don't take this inspiration stuff seriously." I wrestled with that response for a few months. It really hit home hard when the responses were not what I expected from people around me, and on social media. I began doubting the gift, the message, and the messenger. I doubted myself.

Nothing can happen to you that you and God cannot handle together.
Rev. Shaun J. Lee

Only a tiny nugget of doubt was needed to knock the wind out of my aspirations. However, in *true me* fashion, I dusted off my converses and got back on the road to my purpose. I realize that it may not be as easy for everyone to accept my life's work. I also never insinuated it was going to be easy for me, but resilient people do not and will not stop until they achieve their goals.

Prepare yourself for the long haul. You may run out of supplies in the physical realm, but you will experience overflow in the spiritual realm. This means that you will experience some wins. Your wins can be interpreted as gaining more patience, energy, grit, and even your focus for the work that you are doing. You have to remain prayerful and move with faith. You have to trust your spiritual deposits, and not lose sight of the big picture. You are doing this work, on this journey, creating greatness for a reason. As you grow in faith, you will move into spaces that may cause a stir with outsiders and your naysayers. Remember, the public does not need to know if your glass is half empty, half full, or broken. You don't have to broadcast your every move or every decision that you do regarding your life's work and the journey. The "hush-move" isn't necessarily sneaky, it is caution, because of the great work that you are purposed to do. You will give one person credit, and that's the one who gave you the divine revelation, God. *And as Moses lifted up the serpent in the wilderness, even so must the Son of man be lifted—John 3:14.* Don't be deterred by the snakes, or naysayers that come around and hover over you. They have a job to do, but obedience and resilience are your jobs. God has created a way for your win and His glory. He has got you! Press forward toward the mark!

Divine Butterfly Meditation

*Does your prayer life line up
with your purpose?*

Butterfly Reflection

Chapter 5

PATIENCE

While on this journey of self-growth and purpose, there is a skill that you will need to master: patience. You will be tried again and again by people close to you and those who may even matter in your big picture. That skill requires much patience. You need to build a patience muscle and exercise it every day or as often as you can. Let me suggest that you adopt this daily inspirational mantra: "*I am learning patience on the journey.*" Patience builds resilience. Daily mantras also help you build the patience muscle, and it will eventually yield discernment.

The road to success will get rough at times. In fact, more times than you will have the capacity to endure. But if you are patient, you will get to your destination in God's allotted time. Trust me, I know about the timelines that we create and the benchmarks that we have in place for ourselves and our wins. Sometimes, that is for us and not for God. If this life work journey is to your purpose, then there is a schedule that you know nothing about. You just have to exercise faith and be patient. You need to be able to hear what is going on around you, especially if it is related to your work, you will begin to experience a keen sense of hearing. Think Superman's hearing skills coupled with discernment. You will not only hear what's happening in the natural realm but in the spiritual realm as well. Is this conversation a divine encounter or someone getting close to trip you up? You need to hear yourself think— are you exercising self-sabotage or are you grinding according to plan? This is critical because God may have some instructions for you, but if you are too busy being busy, you are most likely to MISS OUT.

This may be the time when you experience burnout and feel as though you have no endurance because you have done all you can and the results do not look as anticipated. Your

38

conversations with God become an argument, and you question everything. Is this time wasted, was this deposited into my spirit? Is this really my life's purpose? Those are the internal fights. But then, there is the external warfare when people around you express their thoughts and share advice about how you should work or maybe move on from what you are doing. Patience will not be something that pops up. You will be in a place of brokenness.

A place of brokenness can be likened to a personal Gethsemane moment of sorts. Gethsemane means an instance or place of great suffering. Most of us learned about Gethsemane in Religious Education classes. It is known as the place where Jesus spent the last night with the disciples before his crucifixion. It is the place where he prayed for a pass on his life's work, his purpose journey. The culminating event was happening and his time was limited.

> *"...My Father, if it is possible, may this cup be taken from me. Yet not as I will, but as you will."*
> *Matthew 26: 39*

If I were in Jesus' place, let me be super transparent with you, there would have been a different ending. In fact, I doubt if any of us would go through with sacrificing our lives as Jesus did for the world. Our prayer would sound something like this, "Um... they good. I changed my mind. I do not want to take the fall for all of those people." Instead, Jesus prayed for strength until sweat turned into blood. He surrendered to the Will of God because He knew that the purpose of His life's journey was for this moment. Can you imagine the intensity of that moment? Knowing that your purpose is at hand and the most grueling part of the journey is upon you, and there is nothing you can do to change it. Have you ever given thought to what you would do? Your culminating event will not be death, but it's your end game.

Your Gethsemane moment (however it shows up for you) is a time when you pray with all of your might; with all of your heart, and without ceasing. Even when you know, it will not work out in your favor. The hurt, the anger, and the mistrust will cause you to buckle and want to give up. It can also be the time when you decide to nail all of your issues to the cross and ask God to move on your behalf, but, only if it is His will. The prayer during Jesus' moments in Gethsemane gives you an idea of how bad the situation was.

Jesus had the disciples or his squad with Him when he entered the garden. He asked them to stay up, but they all fell asleep at the most crucial time that He needed them. One even turned on Him. This does not mean that the squad was wacky, they took on the ride-or-die role of humans. Your personal squad will get tired; they have their own issues to deal with; they want their dreams to become a reality, they will fall asleep. That does not mean they are not with you. If you received a call from your doctor's office stating that they found some abnormal results in your tissue test, whom would you call? Who are the friends that will show up at the doctor's office just to hold your hand? Who are the friends that will take your kids so that you won't have to worry about their safety? Who do you trust with your funds? That's your squad. Choose your squad (disciples) wisely as they will endure the Gethsemane moments with you and you with them. They will enter the Garden and stand by your side, flaws and all. They will not be perfect, no one is, but they should believe in you. They should have a healthy relationship with you. It would not be wise to have folks who are not totally in your corner, praying for you at your moment of surrender. That can lead to a ball of confusion because the heart is not right. Prayerfully choose your squad. Keep them lifted in prayer at all times and ask that they do the same for you.

Divine Butterfly Meditation

Create a "meditative prayer" for those moments.

Butterfly Reflection

Chapter 6

CHOICES

Have you ever experienced a weird sensation to walk away from friendships, relationships, and even family members? The feeling was of discomfort, but not just any kind, it was a feeling that resonated from your core. Everything within you said "walk away" or "stay away," you cannot and will never be able to explain the feeling or the urgency, but you did react accordingly. That is called discernment. You have to make a choice: whether you will listen to it or let it pass because you are overthinking things.

You have to develop your spirit of discernment or perceptiveness while on the journey of your purpose. It will help you make hard decisions and at times, bypass some speed bumps and traps. Discernment will help you recognize the negative culprits that will try to take up residence in your space. It will also help with the challenges that you will encounter while on the journey because as time goes on, you will easily recognize potential threats, a far cry from actually being in the thick of things and having to work your way out.

As you discern the challenges, you begin to speak and move differently. You will start making wise decisions that will benefit your growth. You will not frequent the same places you did in the past. You will become very conservative with sharing information about your plans and actions. Does it sound like I am suggesting you become secretive? Maybe! I also call it being cautious about who and how you share this purpose journey's itinerary.

Now, there are times you will choose to disregard the feeling and continue with your routines; as a consequence, the issue will intensify because you have allowed it to fester in your space. The irritation of this negative spirit will become overwhelming and eventually you will have to act on it. However, since you were not quick to act, you may have a hard time explaining yourself. Some of you may chuckle at this point and think "you do not have to explain yourself to anyone." Sometimes, the explanation and reconciliation are with yourself.

Do you remember a scene from a movie, The Matrix when Morpheus showed up and gave Thomas Anderson the option of choosing between two pills? He is naturally a Blue Pill because that is the normal existence of all who are connected to the Matrix. He was a computer programmer at a software company, and he was also a hacker that used the alias NEO. Hacking was his hobby that afforded him extra cash. As time went on, he noticed that something was off balance with the world around him. It was time to follow the white rabbit. Upon meeting Morpheus, an offer was made that would change the course of his life. The offer was 'choice' - The Red Pill and the Blue Pill. Morpheus said *"If you take the blue pill, the story ends: you wake up and believe whatever you want to believe. You take the red pill, and you stay in Wonderland, and I will show you how deep the rabbit goes."* Society believes that the pills represent the choices that we make between knowledge, freedom, the painful truth of reality; as well as, falsehoods and blissful ignorance.

This journey that you are on is your personal Matrix: you see the needs of humanity and understand that you have been gifted and purposed to pour into them and make them better than they have ever been. You acknowledge that some live in a simulated universe—a sort of virtual reality and they do not have access to choice. The culprits holding them hostage come in the form of music, reality television, movies, and even books. They get caught up in the lifestyle of a curated show or song. It is as though they take a drug and become addicted to the trappings of a non-realistic lifestyle. You are susceptible to the same mind traps that they experience. No one is exempt because our culture is saturated with these crazy choices.

There is another culprit that has more power than anyone or anything else. This culprit is (can be) yourself: yes, we are known to set our own traps and fall right into them. There are usually no choices with this one. It is all about you.

Beware of Self-Sabotage.
It is debilitating

You can avoid this by learning more about yourself and your habits.

Conduct a SWOT Analysis on yourself. We tend to do these for businesses and for individuals who want to work with us, but we rarely do personal SWOTS. You may already know your strengths and some opportunities, but what are your weaknesses and threats? What and who do they look like? Take some serious time for yourself to work in this analysis as it will yield useful information on how you should navigate on this journey.

Once you learn how to deal with them, you will acknowledge that some challenges are growth pills, some are death pills, and some are power pills.

In 2003, I visited Atlanta to attend a conference themed:

"Spirit and Truth." It was a life-changing experience for me. I had my personal Neo experience where the blue pill and the red pill were presented to me—in a figurative sense of course. No one gave me pills nor did I seek them out. The event changed the course of my life forever because I not only learned much about myself, I received the instructions for my life's purpose assignment during that conference. I mean every aspect of my life work was laid down for me. One of the lecturers at the conference shared a lesson that goes thus: "When God created the animals, he did not call the bird, mouse, and He did not call the wolf, rabbit. Each animal had a name, and they were called as such. More importantly, they responded to their given names and not one that was given to them by a random person." Why is that important? The first part of doing the life's work is knowing who you are and what you are about? How do you make choices? But more importantly, are you taking the blue or red pill?

Learn about the things that are good for you, things that are bad for you, and things that will stop a superficial infection before it spreads. You will encounter thickets and thorns and rocky terrains while on this journey. Call the things in your life what they are and not what you wish them to be. If you have trouble recognizing it, STOP - ASSESS IT - ACT ON IT. Call things as you see them and be mindful of this at all times. Treat them like vitamins that you choose to take every day. You have a choice of three pills that you can take every morning as you begin your day. It all depends on what you allow deposited inside you by society, friends, or your force of habit.

Let's name these pills as follows:

Growth Pill*: Benchmarks that pop up to show you how far you have come.*

Death Pill*: Drain life and energy from you.*

This is a major distraction as it can kill the dream completely.

Power Pills*: Boost to carry on in your purposeful journey.*

Don't let your habits or people slow down your growth process. You are the master of your fate

Divine Butterfly Meditation

What 'pills' have you noticed in your immediate space?

Butterfly Reflection

Chapter 7

DISAPPOINTMENTS

You acting all brand new, keep it real. "Words of hater."

"Finally, it is about time! I was just waiting for you to get on with it."

You will hear those words from the people who have always been in your corner and have benefitted from the purpose work that you have been doing before you even knew what it was. And then there are the others: the ones who think it is all a waste of time. Have you noticed that some people become very judgmental when you share the big life changing idea with them?

I remember uploading a post on social media over a year ago. It mentioned new material that was coming soon from my company. I am not the one to release items for sale, so when I did do one thing, folks knew that nothing was coming behind that anytime soon. A non-supporter, someone I've known for years, someone that I have supported a lot of times commented on my post, 'about time.' That set me off my rails. I had the attitude of 'how dare you, who do you think you are.'

I caught myself after some time. I needed to remind myself that this person owes me nothing and it's easy to be on the sidelines calling audible

Folks will disappoint you, turn against you, talk about you (true/untrue), and turn others against you the day you embark on this purpose journey.

Sometimes your destiny's purpose is not in the natural sight of folks, and it may never be. They will have much commentary on what they think you should do, moreover, how best to get it done. Don't react, let them talk and comment as they feel. You are putting in the work.

You were given the vision; you must do the work regardless of what is happening around you. Always keep in mind that only you can interpret your vision.

Friendships, work relationships, love relationships, and non-committed relationships all take work to make them great. And when everyone works towards the same end goal, it can be a "grand old time."

It is the same with your purpose's work. Those who are with you, your squad, will help you get to your end goal. Now, if you couple that with your power pills and your growth pills, you will be a force to reckon with in the world.

This winning experience can create a fork on the road of the journey. Especially with friends and family. Folks can have a great relationship with you until the relationship hits a speed bump and everything goes haywire.

When you get to that point, it should not trigger "the end of the ride." You have to be patient. When you are working towards this purpose, you are very sensitive to attitudinal changes, and you will be quick to end it all.

I cannot tell you the number of people I had to cut off because I was always *in my feelings*. I found myself always depositing my resources into relationships but was unable to withdraw. I could not depend on folks. They never had time or resources to give in return; in the end, it was a bust. I felt that they were dismissive of my goals or that they did not really care if I was going to be successful—I was a total fussy mess. Some of the cuts were for my good, and other were just causalities of circumstance. You cannot cry over spilled milk; acknowledge your shortcomings and carry on. Keep your mind on what is important and move accordingly.

Assess the situation as there may be many variables that can cause agitation in your work and movements. Someone may be going through a rough patch; it is in times like these that you have to get some tea and get over some stuff. Start with the BIG3 that always show up without invitation:

*Ego   *Impatience   *Jealousy

Divine Butterfly Meditation

Create your personal "recharge" mantra.

Butterfly Reflection

Chapter 8

I AM...

Who am I to do this work? Who gives me validation?
(Doubting self)

Moses was tasked with his life's work to lead the Israelites out of bondage in Egypt and into the promised land of milk and honey. Moses had some reservations about this job that was placed on him. As I stated in the intro, you will have some reservations, and I know that I did when I started my life's work and while I am on this journey of writing this book. His personal question was "who am I to do this work?' It's not a sign of weakness or ego, it's being humble and transparent. In this space of humility, we are molded into our best selves in order to put forth our best work.

Moses also knew that Pharaoh would doubt him as well. They grew up as brothers in the Palace. They went to the same parties, went to the same schools, they hung out with the same friends while growing up. So his main question was "who am I that I should go to Pharaoh and bring the Israelites out of Egypt?" I am quite sure that if I were in Moses' shoes, I would have many more questions before that one, but, Moses was going back home, and he knew his brother was not going to play nice. Moses had more questions, "Suppose I go to the Israelites and say to them, 'The God of your fathers has sent me to you,' and they ask me, 'What is his name?' Then what shall I tell them?" Earlier in the book in the chapter called 'Clarity,' I mentioned that you should curate what folks say about you and how they say it. You never want someone else to share their own personal perspective that can be misinterpreted and turn people away.

When Moses asked, 'who am I to tell them sent me?" God replied Moses by saying, *"I AM WHO I AM. This is what you are to say to the Israelites: 'I AM has sent me to you.'"* God also said to Moses, *"Say to the Israelites, 'The LORD, the God of your fathers—the God of Abraham, the God of Isaac and the God of Jacob—has sent me to you.'"* He continued *"This is my name forever; the name you shall call me from generation to generation." (Exodus 3:14-15)*

Dictation! Tell them what you want them to say, and how to say it. God gave Moses the verbiage to use when talking to Pharaoh and his men. You should follow this rule of thumb and give them the verbiage.

I AM WHO I AM...

(Exodus 3:14)

I am not saying that you are God, but I want you to follow His example. Be very clear about who you are and what you are about. First thing is to learn a handful of descriptive words that define your lifestyle and your work. Then you craft the narrative according to your personality: is it austere, comical, soft, a story. You will know what to do or create a few scenarios.

You should have a dictionary, a thesaurus and a notebook for this exercise. The first question that you should ask yourself is: "What is my temperament?" The Merriam-Webster dictionary defines temperament as characteristic or habitual inclination or mode of emotional response. What characteristics have you noticed to be consistent in your life throughout the years? Are you a nervous nelly, do you have a type A personality? Are you witty or grumpy? Think Seven Dwarfs from the Snow White stories. Each dwarf had a personality and was named for it. Which personality traits do you have? Alternatively, are you all seven? Take the time to assess the quirks of the person that you see in the mirror. You must be very honest with yourself about who YOU are as a person, friend, child, parent, et cetera. Acknowledge your pet peeves, as they too must be listed in order to see what is working for or against you.

Are you cynical, are you snarky? Do those attributes work for you and what you are about? Don't forget: we are all guilty of projecting our feelings without a word being said. One thing you want to avoid is someone receiving a subconscious jab as you speaking words of love into their space. No one wants to feel as though they are being mocked. Once people feel slighted or interpret your "love" as condescending, they stop listening and are turned off from you. This assessment shows you what you project subconsciously and where you are bold with your words.

When you are finished with that assessment, analyze the strong words. Use them in a descriptive sentence about yourself.

"Karen can be clandestine, even in a crowded room.' The word clandestine has many meanings and can be broken down in so many ways, but I dictate which definitions goes with that statement by the way that I move and talk about myself.

Once you have completed the exercise of pulling words that best describe you and the work that you do, use those new words to describe yourself in a conversation. Teach people to use those words when talking about you, whether casually or professionally. Get a thesaurus to find words that accurately fits your description.

Sometimes, you have to encourage yourself with power words.

Divine Butterfly Meditation

List five adjectives that best describe you.

- *Use them frequently.*
- *Teach others to use them when talking about you.*
- *Add them to your bio.*

Butterfly Response

Chapter 9

ATTITUDE

Having a positive attitude can be a magical elixir during your journey: You can get a rush from being positive, it's like drinking an energy drink when you get tired. You develop a rhythmic cadence in your step that reflects the bubbly energy. This positive disposition can prompt you to create a new product or even take a massive leap of faith on an idea that you have been mulling over. At some point on your journey, you will get tired. I don't want you to think everything is fun every day. That's furthest from the truth: there will be times when you will feel tired and dismayed, and you will even get to the point of "I Quit," but, that's a moment that will soon pass. Don't allow the down times to consume you.

Embarking on your purpose journey to do your life's work likens a trek up Mt. Everest. You have to condition your body and your mind to embark on the journey. As you go further and learn more about yourself and the work, you can sometimes get lost in your own ego and thoughts be they good or bad. More importantly, it's booby trapped for others to get into your head.

Be steadfast! Don't let folks fool you into thinking that you will not get to the brink of abandoning ship. The thought and the act are very different. Having a good disposition may require you to be patient and committed.

Embrace a "positive attitude lifestyle." Create an imaginary tool belt like Superman or Supergirl. Fill it with personal inspirations, music, books, friends, and maybe good wine.

Acknowledge the good in all scenarios. When life throws those curve balls at you and nothing seems to go the way you need or want it to go, or when the situation is grim, try as hard as you can to see or acknowledge the "good" side of it. You are not ignoring the bad that has happened; you are choosing to focus on the good in order to keep going. Your positive attitude can actually serve as a trampoline that will spring you back into the game.

Practice an attitude of giving. What you give can be in the form of your time, talent, or money. Pour into others without expecting anything in return—it is like making deposits into your karmic bank that will accumulate for that rainy day.

Exercise an attitude of gratitude. Always be thankful for the situation, whether good, bad, or indifferent because there is always a lesson to be learned. Be gracious to those who help you—shower them with gifts, and acts of kindness.

In my early twenties, I was referred to as "the loose cannon." It took less than a millisecond to set me off. I was not here for this bit or that bit. If you wanted to see the head and eye rolls of an aggressive person, just take me to the left. Well, I learned (not too quickly) that my attitude was a major roadblock to my success. Folks just assumed the wrongdoing was my fault and I was blamed. Sometimes my explanations fell on deaf ears. It was my entire fault. I still blame it on my only child status. I went to a same-sex high school, I was tiny, and I had no one to defend me. So, I had to develop this defense mechanism that would not only scare bullies but also, keep me safe. I had no problem throwing hands and talking smack

As I jumped into my thirties, I learned not to be as loud, but to perfect my wrath. Well, in my forties, I still have tendencies, and it shows up at times.

However, now, the response from others is usually, "who messed with her? Who would take her to that place? Folks better act like they know she is consistent!"

Being consistent can save your reputation.

I meditate daily to "embrace my positive attitude lifestyle" and not fall into the traps of negativity.

There are occasions when that I use music to guide my meditative process. I have certain songs that take me into a zone where I can relax and focus on the moment. Let me give you a visual of how I set the atmosphere and get into the session. First, I burn or spray some lavender aroma into the air, then, queue my playlist of at least three or four songs of the same genre and lastly, I use prayer beads to keep my concentration with my mantras.

Music is important for me because it not only keeps me abreast of the time, but it helps with my breathing sequence. There are times when I have one song on repeat throughout the session. One of my favorite and most used songs for meditation is a classic hymn written in the 18th century. The song is 'Come Thou Fount of Every Blessing" written by Pastor Rob Robinson. I particularly like the version sung by the Mormon Tabernacle Choir. The lyrics reference a verse in the bible, 1 Samuel 7:12, which notes that the prophet Samuel "took a stone, and set it between Mizpeh and Shen, and named of it Ebenezer; stone of help. This meant, "Hitherto hath the Lord helped us." When I listen to this song during meditation, one particular verse takes resets all my buttons, reboots my energy to work harder in my purpose. That verse reads: "Prone to wander, Lord I feel it, Prone to leave the Lord I love..." This is fitting for meditation because it is my sacred time that should be spent with God. Let me say this, my mind will wander to the upcoming meeting, conversation or event that I have to attend to.

> *Prone to wander, Lord I feel it,*
> *Prone to leave the God I love,*
> *Come Thou Fount of Every Blessing*
> *Pastor Rob Robinson*

For you, it may be the kids, dinner, family, work or even something regarding this purpose journey. Add something that will keep you grounded for a period of time as you meditate.

The attitude that you take into meditation will dictate what you get out of it. If you take the time to curate the moment, you will get more out of it than you bargained for.

Divine Butterfly Meditation

Create Meditation Mantra:

(a) Public one that can be recited aloud if needed

(b) Personal one that is meant for your quiet meditation.

Butterfly Reflection

Chapter 10

NO ORDINARY-NESS

ORDINARY: *'ôrdn͵erē/adjective: with no special or distinctive features; normal*

Have you ever taken the time to assess all of your talents? Is there a list from pre-teen years when you wrote down your future occupation and why? Have you ever prayed about the gifts that are naturally yours and actually paid attention to them?

You have to win your gifts and talents, master them, and manifest your destiny.

You must accept that fact that you are more than enough. Know that you are more than just normal—you are fearfully and wonderfully made. There is no "ordinary-ness" in your world—own these words. You may sing and dance like everyone else, but what flare do you add to it? Is it that you can hold a note and riff until the birds start chirping or are you off key and could care less because you feel the music in your soul? There is nothing ordinary about you.

You may be asking: "what are my gifts and talents and how can I identify them?" Your talents are the skills that you have that came about naturally. You just knew how to sing, play that instrument, speak with conviction, or even cook that good meal. Your gifts for the sake of this book, they are the supernatural talents that came with your soul. They are the special ability of capacity; a natural endowment. Were you a natural craftsperson, administrator or even a natural speaker? Things that you didn't go to school to do, there was no apprenticeship, you just did it. Those are gifts.

Have you ever seen a child actor or singer that is just "au naturel" when they dive into their craft? There are some things that people cannot take from you unless you give it away. Your gifts are just that—they were all tailored for your lifestyle and your journey. Who would think that some folks have a gift just to love other people? It cannot be explained, and they can overlook the ills of others and just love on them.

I was having breakfast with a friend, and the conversation was about family and how people love differently. He has a twin brother, and they could not be more different than night and day. Then the topic of the capacity to love people, in general, yielded a funny scenario. His twin brother can love anyone despite of their murky past or present. His love is 'au natural.' Not his love language, his capacity is such. Whereas my friend can love you on Monday and think about it on Friday. It's not about being selfish, but it's about how people use their gifts and talents to impact the world. Both men are unique, but there is nothing ordinary about who they are as individuals. One can heal the world while the other can ruin someone's world.

"Hey, you are a natural."
Ordinary just won't do!

You have individuals like Oprah who can speak life into a person without ever knowing who they are or where they are. She has the ability to draw from the universe the words that are needed to soothe and to connect the disjointed dots in people's lives. There is nothing ordinary about her, she's the gift that she has kept on giving. I am not referring to financial status in the world. I am referring to her status in the realm of depositing and engaging others to do the same.

When you have the ability to shift the earth off its axis, you cannot sit on that gift. Think about it, people who have the power to create wars do so because they are fearless and they believe in their power. Believe in your personal power, know that if you have been blessed with a gift or talent, it is yours to use.

Don't make the mistake of attaching yourself to someone else's talents and gifts because you want to see them succeed. You are not the next Whitney or Gladys, and you are not the next Beyoncé. You are your present self and the moment to strike is now so that you can be the best you! You are enough, and there is nothing ordinary about you.

Take your time and assess yourself and be very critical of what you can consider your gifts and talents as opposed to something you just do.

Divine Butterfly Meditation

YOU are FABULOUS!

Butterfly Reflection

Chapter 11

TIMING

One would assume that a surfer would not dare go into the ocean when storms are on the horizon. However, the ocean is dynamic, and it is constantly changing. For that reason, surfers who can quickly and efficiently surf through ocean tides put themselves in the right spot—they are the ones who will score maneuvers of the highest quality.

On the other hand, inexperienced surfers who are not well acquainted with the sport, are rarely in the right place at the right time. As a result, they have a rough time catching great waves. Knowing how to read waves is essential to surfers, it leads to more time spent surfing and less time hanging out on the shoulder watching others have all the fun. This guide offers a crash course in this fine art within the sport.

Like surfers, we have to learn how to get a "good run," especially when the storms are upon us; we have to learn how to ride situations out. Adopt the attitude of the inexperienced surfer, hang out on the shoulders for a while. Don't throw in the towel, be observant. Experienced surfers analyze the tides. They analyze the shape of the wave and how long it takes to develop. They also sit and watch other surfers. If you take the time to sit and watch the people in your space, you may learn a thing or two about handling disappointments, failure, and stress. More importantly, you can watch other people win and celebrate with them.

Don't run from the storm and disappointments. Work through them and fashion your core so that you can handle the next storm. There will be flash storms here and there to keep you on your toes, but when you learn to deal with them, you consequently build up your endurance. There will be many encounters with these storms while on your journey.

My major storm was riding the New York City subway, and

getting stuck in the tunnels—talk about anxiety attacks. My stomach drops, my heartbeat races, my palms get sweaty, and my hands quivered. The longer I am in the tunnel, the worse it gets: my breathing becomes labored, and I began to panic. That is a storm for the books, and I had to endure this at least five times a month. I took measures to help me with this issue.

I had a *Past-Life Regression (PLR)* therapy done. Past-Life Regression is a technique that uses hypnosis to recover what practitioners believe are memories of one's past lives or incarnations. Past-Life Regression is typically undertaken either in pursuit of a spiritual experience or a psychotherapeutic setting.

I did PLR because I needed to know why I had issues with these tunnels. Mind you, I have been taking the subway by myself on a consistent basis since the age of fourteen. I learned that the background of my phobia of closed spaces had to do with a traumatic situation that happened in a past lifetime. I also learned that the anxiety issues become overwhelming because I am also fearful of what will happen to others if I don't do my purpose work. What I learned made sense and it also allowed me to create these coping techniques for the experience.

I know my time limit: I am fine for the first three minutes and then it is downhill from there. Before I venture to the trains, I make sure that my phones are charged, and my portable power banks charged to their maximum capacity. I also make certain that the charging cord is in my bag. I used to find myself with either a charger or the cord and never both. I have two games on my phone that I play; and lastly, I have specific playlists for "situations." I choose the appropriate one at any given time, and I try to get lost in the moment.

Even after my PLR, I still suffer from anxiety, but not as bad as it used to be. I can sit in the tunnels a "little" longer than I used to in past months. I have acknowledged the persistent storm in my life, but I surf still. Although quite often, I fall off the board, but I always get back on and ride it out. Literally!

Think about timing your movements in different situations. So for me, I would automatically look at the time on my watch or phone as soon as the train stops in the tunnel. I know that at the five-minute mark, I have a problem. I have to pull my coping devices to get me over because at some point I am going to lose it. I will experience an anxiety attack. It is like on a beautiful summer day with your favorite surfboard, there are a few things that you should be mindful of always:

- **When to ride the wave.**

- **What waves can take you out.**

- **When to get out of the water.**

All of these things will help get to your end goal of a safe and fun-filled day at the beach. Not a thing is different when compared to LIFE.

Divine Butterfly Meditation

Do you have grit?

Butterfly Reflection

Chapter 12

SACRIFICES

There is an old saying: "You have to give a little in order to gain a little." Be willing to make major sacrifices in order to bring your dreams to fruition. You may have to sacrifice time with your family and friends; you may have to sacrifice vacations and dinners out with friends, but it will be worth it in the end.

> *Joy is making sacrifices for your life's purpose journey.*

There's something to be said about rolling up your sleeves and getting your hands dirty. Doing the work required to succeed should not be beneath you. Long gone are the days of Lords and Serfs where someone does the work, and another gets the credit.

Lend a hand to someone else that is on his or her path of purpose when you can. This allows you to build community support and partnerships. You never know when you will be the beneficiary of good tiding from such selfless tasks.

If you are apprehensive about this talking point, take the time to do some research on individuals who have made sacrifices to realize their purpose. It is a common practice, and it serves as a stamp on your passport for this journey.

SOAR!

Divine Butterfly Meditation

What are your "Life Goals"?

*How are you working
on these goals?*

Butterfly Reflection

TAKEAWAYS

Light working is difficult. Knowing that you are purposed to pour into the spirit of others can be daunting. No one ever said that the journey would be an easy one and if they do say it, it's a lie. Stay grounded knowing that you are doing what you have been purposed to bring balance in the universe.

Allow me to help in your meditative sessions. When you are totally burnt out and don't really want to share with anyone, meditate. Take the time to sit, walk or even drive and focus on one of the terms listed below.

Converse with yourself, ask hard questions and formulate the answers. It is not crazy; it is part of self-preservation and awareness. (See example below)

- Get out of your own way when doing life's work.

  o Am I in my own way?

  o Am I over reacting?

  o What am I doing wrong?

- Invest time into your work and your personal growth.

  o Take vacations or stay-cations to recharge or reboot your creative juices.

  o Implement 'creative hours' to work. That is time allotted for business, no personal calls or activities.

- o Engage in social activities that are directly related to the work that you do.

- You are enough.

- Be content in your spirit.

- Invest in your talents.

  - o What additional skills do you need to increase your success ratio?

  - o Find classes through your local SBS that will help you build your net worth.

  - o Volunteer at events that will expose you and your brand to potential partners or sponsors.

- Build with like-minded individuals.

  - o Who's in the circle that helps you grow as a person?

  - o Is the inspirational 'pour' equal amongst friends or acquaintances? You should not be the only person depositing into the squad.

Great things don't come without a struggle. Remember that in all good things, the greater the struggle, the greater the impact. Godspeed!

Divine Butterfly Return

Did this book meet your expectations?

ABOUT AUTHOR

Life architect, inspirational motivator, and philanthropist. Karen H. St. Hilaire is a visionary with over 20 years of experience in personal development and strategic consulting.

St. Hilaire is the founder and CEO of Kadence LLC—a strategic solutions consulting firm specializing in personal development and social impact work. Her areas of focus include faith-based initiatives to educational and corporate programs.

Additionally, she is an accomplished author, inspirational motivator, sought-after speaker, and distinguished business strategist committed to investing her talents and expertise to effect positive social change with a global impact.

She currently serves as a Trustee for St. Joseph's High School, Brooklyn, NY; Board Member of Indescribable Gift, Indianapolis, IN; and Board Advisor for Young Enterprising Sisters Inc. Princeton, New Jersey. Karen H. St. Hilaire is a member of Alpha Kappa Alpha Sorority, Inc. currently residing in Brooklyn, NY.

Learn more at www.karensthilaire.com

Thank you for supporting

The Divine Butterfly: Inspiration For Your Journey
To Your Purpose

Pour into the life and purpose of a friend, gift them a copy of this book.

Made in the USA
Middletown, DE
21 September 2017